SCHOLASTIC

Reading without realising

Reading signs, lists, letters and more

DOG FOOD

Brenda Whittle and Heidi Jayne

For ages 3–5

Authors
Brenda Whittle
and Heidi Jayne

Editor
Kate Element

Project Editor
Rachel Mackinnon

Series Designer
Anna Oliwa

Designer
Geraldine Reidy

Cover Illustration
Craig Cameron

Illustrations
Debbie Clark

Text © 2007 Brenda Whittle and Heidi Jayne
© 2007 Scholastic Ltd

Designed using Adobe InDesign

Published by Scholastic Ltd
Book End
Range Road
Witney
Oxfordshire
OX29 0YD

www.scholastic.co.uk

Printed by Bell & Bain

2 3 4 5 6 7 8 9   0 1 2 3 4 5 6

British Library Cataloguing-in-Publication Data
A catalogue record for this book is available from the British Library.

ISBN 978-0439-94556-1

Mixed Sources
Product group from well-managed forests and other controlled sources
www.fsc.org Cert no. TT-COC-002769
© 1996 Forest Stewardship Council
FSC

Contents

Discovering reading

Reading environments

Reading around

Reading without realising

Introduction

Reading without realising

Reading without realising is one of a series of books containing 'outside the box' ideas for practitioners working with children in the early years. Children's interests and joy for life form the basis for the activities in this series. The activities build on children's natural instinct to be doing, investigating, making, creating and solving problems. They are designed to excite and stimulate children as they learn through using their senses, being active and thinking for themselves.

But why reading without realising?

The cross-curricular activities in this book are designed to inspire and excite children so that they cannot wait to participate, unaware that they will be learning to read along the way. The activities take the pressure off learning to read by making reading a natural progression in learning which is integral to speaking, listening and writing, rather than a separate hurdle to overcome. Learning to read is a complex process that some children sail through, others find a struggle and some find difficult and dispiriting, leaving them with a feeling of failure at a very early age. To make reading a rewarding and enjoyable experience for all children, carefully planned reading opportunities are embedded into each cross-curricular play activity. This ensures that, without the children realising it, reading is a part of the activity and will entice them into the world of print and books. Children will be learning to read through 'doing', in fun activities set indoors and out. Throughout the book, care is taken to devise lively activities that will appeal to boys and reluctant readers.

Wanting to read

If we can inspire children to want to read, they are well on the way to success. The activities and reading environments in this book are designed to capture the imagination of children, to draw them in and fascinate them so that reading becomes irresistible.

How to use this book

The book is organised into three sections:

● Chapter 1: 'Discovering reading' includes a wide variety of exciting activities that introduce children to the world of print. They learn to recognise letters, link sounds to letters, read words and simple sentences. The activities range from taking on the role of a postal worker in a sorting office to reading words written on shells at the bottom of the sea or taking part in a game show. Children find that print carries meaning and want to find out more.

● Chapter 2: 'Reading environments' provides inspiration and practical advice for making reading areas that children cannot wait to explore. Children participate in making areas where they take part in role play, discovering the world of print, books and rhyme. These areas captivate children and provide new experiences, such as working in a jungle cafe where the customers are animals, repairing toys in a workshop or 'going inside a book' in Giant's world and Bears in the forest. The children step inside a television where they explore different 'zones' and read non-fiction materials. The children's involvement in creating these areas and making them their own, is in itself a valuable learning opportunity. The environments provide a wonderful stimulation for reading and cross-curricular learning over the period of a term. To keep them alive and exciting, change the focus from time to time, introducing a new idea, an unexpected visitor or event.

● Chapter 3: 'Reading around' introduces offbeat starting points for reading to challenge and intrigue children. They 'read the rhythm' as they move to music, learn to read expressions and the messages that their bodies are sending them.

The activities

Planning and learning objectives. Links to the Stepping Stones and Early Learning Goals for Communication, language and literacy (CLL) in the QCA document *Curriculum guidance for the foundation stage* are shown for each activity to aid planning. The activities are all cross-curricular and the main link to one of the other five Areas of Learning is also shown.

Support and extension

Each activity has suggestions for practitioners to adapt or extend the activities according to children's needs and stage of development.

Assessment

Practitioners can assess children against the Stepping Stones and Early Learning Goals shown for each activity. Most of the activities are designed for small groups, enabling practitioners to observe individual children's progress and aid assessment to inform future planning.

Further activities

These provide more suggestions for developing lively activities linked to the main activity.

Play links

Ideas for play linked to the main activity are given to continue the theme into other Areas of Learning, such as opportunities for investigations or role play.

Home links

In order to promote and foster a partnership with parents or carers, a suggestion is given in each activity to link the learning in the setting to that in the home.

Health and safety

When working outside, always check that the area is clean and safe.

Abbreviations
References to Areas of Learning in the QCA document *Curriculum guidance for the foundation stage*:
● Personal, social and emotional development **(PSED)**
● Communication, language and literacy **(CLL)**
● Mathematical development **(MD)**
● Knowledge and understanding of the world **(KUW)**
● Physical development **(PD)**
● Creative development **(CD)**

Discovering reading

Sorting office

The children receive a letter in the setting and think about how it reached them. They pretend to be post workers, sorting letters by street names ready for delivering.

Early readers begin to read and match the street names on the envelopes with the street names in the sorting trays.
More confident readers help to set up their own simple sorting office, based on street names in the locality.

What you need
A letter posted to the children; envelopes, postcards and small packages addressed using street names that can be illustrated such as: Fox Street, Duck Lane, Church Road, Poppy Lane or Bridge Street; shoe boxes labelled with the illustrated street names; a bag labelled 'Post'; rubber bands; 'Post worker' badges.

What to do
● Send a letter to the setting, addressed to the children. Read the letter to them and ask them to think about its journey to the setting

from a postbox near your house. What happened after it was posted? Talk about the fact that the post box is emptied by a postman and the letters are sorted into areas and sent on the next part of their journey. When the postman collects the letters for his round he sorts them into roads so that they are easy to deliver.
● Tell the children that today they will be working in a sorting office, sorting the letters into streets ready for delivering later. Show

Learning objectives
Stepping Stones
● Hear and say the initial sound in words and know which letters represent some of the sounds. **(CLL)**
● Begin to use talk to pretend imaginary situations. **(CLL)**
Early Learning Goals
● Hear and say initial and final sounds in words, and short vowel sounds within words. **(CLL)**
● Use language to imagine and recreate roles and experiences. **(CLL)**

the children the labelled boxes and read the names of the streets together, using the picture cues.

● Give each child a 'Post worker' badge. Show them the bag of letters, cards and small packages. Read some of the names and addresses together and ask the children to help you sort them into the correct boxes, ready for the postman, by looking at the first line of each address. Talk about the fact that the houses have numbers and numbers are also used in the postcode.

● When the letters are all sorted into the correct streets, tell the children to use a large rubber band to hold them together and put the bundles of letters into the postman's bag ready for delivery.

Support and extension

● Work with younger children as their 'assistant', helping them to read and match the street name on the envelope with the street name on the box.

● Older children can tell you the names of streets around the setting and label their own sorting boxes.

Further activities

● Go for a walk in the local area, looking for postboxes. Ask: *How can we tell when a letter will be collected? Is there a collection every day? In which street is the nearest postbox?*

● Write the children's names and addresses on postcards. Ask them to find the postcard with their own name and address on it. Put all of the postcards into the postperson's bag. Ask each child to take a postcard from the bag and read the name of the child on the card. Suggest that they draw a picture or write a simple message and their name on the back, to send to their friend. Provide stamps for the children to put on their cards and take them to a nearby postbox, checking the time they will be collected.

Play link

Provide a tricycle with a basket, letters addressed to different numbers within one street and open cardboard boxes representing houses with numbered doors drawn on them. The children deliver the letters on the tricycle to the correct houses. **(MD)**

Home link

Suggest that parents or carers help their children to learn their own address and let them collect the post and deliver it to the correct person in their house.

Cross-curricular links

Stepping Stone
● Notice what adults do, imitating what is observed and then doing it spontaneously when the adult is not there. **(CD)**

Early Learning Goal
● Use their imagination in role play and stories. **(CD)**

Kings and queens

In this activity the children share picture books about kings and queens and read dressing up cards to help them find the clothes they need in order to get into character.

What you need
A basket or box; dressing up clothes for a king, queen, servant and jester; picture of a jester; two 'thrones' (large chairs covered in fabric); 'If I were king…' photocopiable page 9 enlarged to A3 and mounted on coloured card; picture books about kings and queens.

What to do
● Share the collection of story books with the children, talking about what the characters are doing and the clothes they are wearing. Explain that a jester's role was to entertain with songs, stories and jokes. Talk about the clothes he might wear and show the children a picture. Show the children the clothes in the basket and ask them to say which clothes would be worn by a king, queen, servant or jester.
● Look at the dressing up cards from the photocopiable sheet together and choose one of them. Encourage the children to use the picture cues to help them read the words and then collect together all of the items they will need when dressing up as that character. Read the list again, checking off each item.

Early readers use the picture cues on the dressing up cards to help them find the dressing up items they need.
More confident readers make their own dressing up cards to use when finding items to take on the roles of extra characters.

● Tell the children that you want them each to choose one of the dressing up cards and to read the list of items they will need, before dressing up and pretending to be that character. The king and queen can sit on their thrones.

Support and extension
● Play alongside younger children, reading the card and finding the appropriate dressing up items together.
● Provide dressing up items for additional characters such as a cook or driver and ask older children to write and illustrate their own dressing up cards.

Further activity
● Take photographs of the children when they are in character. (Ensure you get parents' or carers' permission before taking photographs.) Make these into a simple book for the children to read with captions beneath the photos.

Play link
Provide resources for a crown-making workshop. These could include card, scissors, stapler, gold and silver foil, beads, foil shapes, sequins and glue. **(KUW)**

Home link
Encourage the children to borrow a crown and one of the story books about kings and queens to share with their parents or carers.

Learning objectives
Stepping Stones
● Know information can be relayed in the form of print. **(CLL)**
● Understand the concept of a word. **(CLL)**
● Describe main story settings, events and principal characters. **(CLL)**
Early Learning Goals
● Know that print carries meaning and, in English, is read from left to right and top to bottom. **(CLL)**
● Read a range of familiar and common words and simple sentences independently. **(CLL)**
● Listen with enjoyment, and respond to stories. **(CLL)**

Cross-curricular links
Stepping Stone
● Play alongside other children who are engaged in the same theme. **(CD)**
Early Learning Goal
● Use their imagination in imaginative and role play and stories. **(CD)**

If I were king...

The king

The queen

The servant

The jester

Play school

Children become the 'teachers' as they read words to their soft-toy class in a role-play teaching area. They play with high frequency words and can be write their own words on the board.

What you need
Magnetic board; soft toys; brightly coloured box; some or all of the first 45 high frequency words from the National Literacy Strategy (DfES) printed using different fonts onto coloured card and laminated; novelty fridge magnets; pens and pencils; paper; notebooks.

Learning objectives
Stepping Stones
● Understand the concept of a word. **(CLL)**
● Begin to recognise some familiar words. **(CLL)**
● Begin to form recognisable letters. **(CLL)**
Early Learning Goals
● Read a range of familiar and common words and simple sentences independently. **(CLL)**
● Use a pencil and hold it effectively to form recognisable letters, most of which are correctly formed. **(CLL)**

What to do
● Create a role-play teaching area to encourage the children to read and write words. Provide the children with a magnetic board. Add the box of high frequency words and the magnets.
● Arrange the soft toys on a chair for the children to use as the class. Set up an area with assorted pens, pencils and paper to encourage mark-making and writing. Provide notebooks for the children to use as registers.
● Introduce the children to the role play by spending time in the area modelling the role of the teacher reading the words to the class and attaching them to the board with the magnets.

Support and extension
● Provide younger children with a small number of words to read, illustrated with picture cues.

Early readers use picture cues to help them recognise and read words.
More confident readers read high frequency words and use them to make simple sentences.

● Encourage older children to use the word cards to begin to construct and read simple sentences on the magnetic board. Provide blank laminated cards and whiteboard pens to encourage them to write their sentences.

Further activity
● Share a selection of picture books with the children. Ask them to look for any words they recognise and read these. They should then record these words on Post-it Notes. Are any of the words they have written the same as the words on the high frequency word cards?

Play link
Write some key words, or words linked to a particular topic, on a set of coloured cards and laminate. Provide magnetic boards and lower-case magnetic letters to encourage the children to read the words on the cards and then make the words using the magnetic letters. **(CLL)**

Home link
Give children an envelope containing the note from photocopiable page 11 and the 'I can read' cards which are laminated to take home. Encourage parents and carers to help their children collect more words that they can read.

Cross-curricular links
Stepping Stones
● Notice what adults do, imitating what is observed and then doing it spontaneously when the adult is not there. **(CD)**
● Engage in imaginative and role play based on own first-hand experiences. **(CD)**
Early Learning Goal
● Use their imagination in role play. **(CD)**

I can read

Beginning to read

You can help your child learn to read in lots of different ways. Wherever words are used, there is a reading opportunity. Read the names of shops and roads, signs in supermarkets, food packets, menus or bus tickets. The more you read together, the more interest your child will take in the world around them.

Write words that interest your child, on the laminated cards, using a felt-tipped pen and attach the cards to the fridge with magnets. They can be 'easy' or 'hard' words. For example, 'mum', 'dad', 'party', 'aeroplane' or 'hippopotamus'. Try to make reading these words a fun game lasting two or three minutes. When your child can read the words, wipe the cards with a damp cloth and choose new words together.

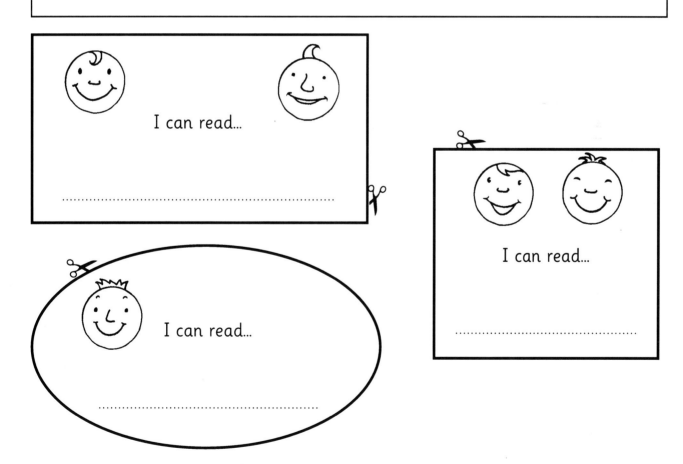

I can read…

I can read…

I can read…

Reading without realising

SCHOLASTIC
www.scholastic.co.uk

Day planner

In this activity children make a washing-line day planner by ordering and reading the names of the activities they will be taking part in.

What you need
A5 card; pens; washing line; pegs; laminator.

What to do
● Ask the children to think of things that they do every day in the setting such as playing outside, having a snack, singing songs and listening to stories.

● List each idea and draw a simple illustration on an A5 card to represent each activity and write the word below. Then laminate the cards.

● Help the children read the words by looking at the picture cues and the initial letters of the words. Explain that some things happen at the same time every day. Tell the children that you want them to make a picture or plan of their day so that they can look at the plan and read what will happen next.

● Together peg the appropriate cards onto the washing line to show the correct order of events for that day. Read the words together, talking about what will happen: first, last, next, after that, before.

● Make time at the start of each session to plan the day in this way to encourage reading, an understanding of the passing of time and to give children a sense of security.

> **Early readers** begin to link sounds to letters and read with support.
> **More confident readers** make and read their own day planners.

Learning objectives
Stepping Stones
● Hear and say the initial sound in words, and know which letters represent some of the sounds. **(CLL)**
● Begin to recognise some familiar words. **(CLL)**
Early Learning Goals
● Hear and say initial and final sounds in words, and short vowel sounds within words. **(CLL)**
● Read a range of familiar and common words and simple sentences independently. **(CLL)**

Support and extension
● Younger children can use photographs to help them plan just three or four activities and read the words with support.
● Older children can discuss and make their own drawings to represent each activity writing the appropriate words below the drawing.

Further activity
● Copy and laminate the cards from photocopiable page 13. Talk to the children about the things they do when they get home. Which things do they do every day? In which order do they do things?

Play link
Talk about the activities the children have taken part in during the day. Mime an action such as building with bricks and ask the children to tell you which activity you are showing. Reverse the roles and guess what the children are miming. **(CD)**

Home link
Encourage parents and carers to involve their children in planning their days when not in the setting. Send home a set of the cards from the photocopiable sheet with a note to parents and carers about how to use them. Invite children to talk about their weekend activities when back in the setting.

Cross-curricular links
Stepping Stone
● Display high levels of involvement in activities. **(PSED)**
Early Learning Goal
● Continue to be interested, excited and motivated to learn. **(PSED)**

My day

Use these cards for reading games and ordering.

I eat my tea.	I play with my toys.	I watch television.
I have a bath.	I read a story.	I brush my teeth.
I say 'night, night'.	I go to bed.	I go to sleep.

Tractor driver

Challenge children to learn how to drive a tractor so that they can earn a 'Tractor driver's' badge and they will soon be reading all the instructions on the control panel.

What you need

Books about vehicles, including some with pictures of the controls; 'In control' photocopiable page 15 – two copies enlarged to A3 one set laminated; 'Tractor driver' badges; large cardboard box; small hoop or circle of thick card; chair; ride-on toys; glue.

What to do

● Share the books about vehicles and ask the children to imagine they are in the cab of a tractor. How will they make the tractor move? Look at the steering wheel and controls inside ride-on toys. Show the children the controls cut out from photocopiable page 15 and read the labels together. Tell the children that you want them to make a control panel to use when they are pretending to learn to drive a tractor.

● Glue the control panel onto the base of a large cardboard box. Cut out a large circle in thick card or use a small hoop for the children to hold as a steering wheel. Place the control panel box in front of a chair to represent the inside of the tractor cab. Read and talk about the different controls. The children can now learn to drive.

● After the children have become familiar

Early readers enjoy driving the tractor and reading the instructions with adult support. **More confident readers** make their own control panels, reading a wider variety of words.

with the words during role play, gather them together and show them the laminated versions of the controls. As part of a matching game tell them that in order to get their tractor driver's badge, they need to be able to read and match the words.

Support and extension

● Assume the role of driving instructor as you teach younger children to 'drive' and help them read the instructions.
● Older children can suggest, draw and label more items to add to the control panel such as fuel, oil, lights, heater.

Further activity

● Adapt the control panel idea to fit in with other topics or stories. For example, make your own controls for a spaceship, ocean liner, train or aeroplane.

Play link

Provide a collection of small-world farm animals, tractors and other farm vehicles to encourage imaginative play. **(CD)**

Home link

Suggest that parents or carers play 'I spy vehicles' with their children on the way to and from the setting and talk about the differences in size and shape of the vehicles they see.

Learning objectives
Stepping Stones
● Show interest in illustrations and print in books and print in the environment. **(CLL)**
● Know information can be relayed in the form of print. **(CLL)**
Early Learning Goal
● Know that print carries meaning and, in English, is read from left to right and top to bottom. **(CLL)**

Cross-curricular links
Stepping Stone
● Play alongside other children who are engaged in the same theme. **(CD)**
Early Learning Goal
● Use their imagination in role play. **(CD)**

In control

left

push

STOP

right

(speedometer)

pull

cold   hot

turn

up

down

Reading without realising

SCHOLASTIC
www.scholastic.co.uk

At the bottom of the sea

Plunge the children's imaginations to the bottom of the sea where they can read watery words and messages.

What you need

Water tray; sand; shells; foam letters; foil confetti; shells and seaweed from 'Sea treasure' photocopiable page 17 enlarged to A3 and laminated; bath books; small-world underwater creatures; food colouring.

Learning objectives
Stepping Stones
● Hear and say the initial sound in words and know which letters represent some of the sounds. **(CLL)**
● Begin to recognise some familiar words. **(CLL)**
Early Learning Goals
● Hear and say initial and final sounds in words, and short vowel sounds within words. **(CLL)**
● Read a range of familiar and common words and simple sentences independently. **(CLL)**

> **Early readers** begin to link sounds to some letters and recognise the first sound in their names.
> **More confident readers** read a range of words and sentences linked to the underwater theme.

What to do
● Put some sand and shells in the water tray and fill it with coloured water. Add some shiny foil confetti, small-world underwater creatures, foam letters, bath books and the laminated shells and seaweed from the photocopiable sheet.
● Tell the children that you want them to imagine that they live at the bottom of the sea in a wet and watery world. Encourage them to play imaginatively and talk about the underwater scene.
● Collect a handful of the foam letters and ask the children to tell you the sound of each letter. Ask them to write their own names using the letters. Read the words on the laminated shells together. Can the children make these words in the tray using the foam letters? Discover the messages written on the seaweed and ask

the children to read these to you and answer the questions.

Support and extension
● Younger children can use the foam letters to find the first letter of their own names and the initial sounds of the items in the sea.
● Invite older children to write messages on fish shapes that can be laminated and left in the sea for others to read.

Further activity
● Make and laminate a simple underwater book with pages in the shape of starfish. Invite the children to draw and label a sea creature on each page. Hide the book at the bottom of the sea for the children to find and read.

Play link
Provide lengths of shiny fabric, 'treasure' and underwater stories such as *The Rainbow Fish* by Marcus Pfister (North-South Books) to encourage imaginative play and enjoyment of books. **(CD)**

Home link
Suggest that parents buy a set of inexpensive foam letters to add to bath time fun. Children can use the letters to write words on the sides of the bath or on themselves.

Cross-curricular links
Stepping Stone
● Play alongside other children who are engaged in the same theme. **(CD)**
Early Learning Goal
● Use their imagination in imaginative and role play and stories. **(CD)**

Sea treasure

sand

shells

fish

octopus

treasure chest

crab

starfish

Can you find some shells?

Where is the treasure?

Is the water cold?

Can you swim?

Can you write some words?

Reading without realising

 **SCHOLASTIC**
www.scholastic.co.uk

Lucky dip

In this outdoor activity, children take a card from a lucky dip and read the instruction that tells them which action to use to move around a circle.

What you need
A set of laminated lucky dip cards from 'Dip into words' photocopiable page 19; bucket of polystyrene packing chips; chalk; laminator.

Early readers begin to read words with adult support.
More confident readers write their own instruction cards for others to read.

What to do
● Draw a large circle on a hard surfaced play area. Write START and draw an arrow to show the direction you want the children to follow around the circle. Hide the laminated lucky dip cards from the photocopiable sheet in the bucket of polystyrene chips and place in the centre of the circle.
● Tell the children that they are going to play a game called 'Lucky dip'. They should stand in the middle of the circle and take it in turns to pull a card from the lucky dip bucket. They read the card aloud and follow the instruction, completing one full circuit of the circle with the rest of the group following them and copying their actions. The children then return to the centre of the circle and another child has a turn.

Learning objectives
Stepping Stones
● Know information can be relayed in the form of print. **(CLL)**
● Begin to recognise some familiar words. **(CLL)**
Early Learning Goal
● Read a range of familiar and common words and simple sentences independently. **(CLL)**

Support and extension
● Limit the number of instruction cards for younger children and read the cards with them.
● Older children can make their own more detailed instruction cards, for example, *Hop five times, Walk very slowly* or *Run fast* and add these to the lucky dip for others to read.

Further activity
● Set up a Funsport area to include available equipment such as a slide, tunnel, stepping stones and balancing beams. Make cards for the Funsport lucky dip, for example, *Go down the slide, Crawl through the tunnel, Walk along the beam.* Award the children stickers such as, *I can slide* or *I can balance,* when they complete an activity.

Play link
Encourage the children to join in with action songs and rhymes, such as 'Five Little Speckled Frogs', 'The Hokey-cokey' or 'Here We Go Round the Mulberry Bush'. **(CD)**

Home link
Leave a set of the lucky dip cards available for children to read to their parents or carers when they collect them from the setting.

Cross-curricular links
Stepping Stone
● Move in a range of ways, such as slithering, shuffling, rolling, crawling, walking, running, jumping, skipping, sliding and hopping. **(PD)**
Early Learning Goal
● Move with confidence, imagination and in safety. **(PD)**

run	walk	skip
jump	hop	jog
dance	march	stamp
tiptoe	crawl	side-step

SCHOLASTIC

www.scholastic.co.uk

Gift wrap studio

Children work in a gift wrap studio making hand-printed wrapping paper. They print with foam letters, recognising the sounds and names of the letters as they work.

What you need

Foam letters; A3 paper; ready-mixed paints; brushes; selection of gift wrap that incorporates greetings; laminated cards from 'All wrapped up' photocopiable page 21.

What to do

● Show the children the gift wrap and talk about when and why we give presents. Examine the different designs and read the greetings.

● Tell the children that they will be working in a 'gift wrap studio' where they will be making very expensive hand-printed wrapping paper. They will be using the foam letters to print designs because the paper will be used for wrapping books. Ask: *Why would a design based on letters be appropriate?*

● Sort through the foam letters with the children, asking them to identify any that they recognise by sound or name. Can they find the letters that make up their names? Show the children how to paint the undersides of the letters and press firmly onto the paper to make a design. Ask them to choose the colours they think will make the best design.

● When the designs are completed, invite the children to look at the letter cards from photocopiable page 21 and match any of these letters with the letters on their gift wrap. Help them to identify the letter sounds and names.

> **Early readers** learn to recognise the initial sounds in their names. **More confident readers** use an alphabet strip to check which letters of the alphabet they know.

Support and extension

● Encourage younger children to hear the initial sound in their names, find the corresponding letter and use this in printing their design.

● Older children can use the alphabet strip to see how many letters they recognise.

Further activity

● Ask the children to choose a favourite book, wrap it in their own gift wrap and pretend to give it to their favourite teddy as a gift. Encourage the child to open it with teddy and share the book.

Play link

Provide a selection of inexpensive gift wrap designed for specific occasions, gift tags, scissors, sticky tape and string. Pretend one of the teddies is having a birthday and encourage the children to choose an item from around the setting to wrap as a 'gift'. **(KUW)**

Home link

Ask parents or carers to spend a few minutes with their children looking at and reading greetings cards when out shopping.

> **Learning objectives**
> **Stepping Stones**
> ● Distinguish one sound from another. **(CLL)**
> ● Hear and say the initial sound in words, and know which letters represent some of the sounds. **(CLL)**
> **Early Learning Goal**
> ● Link sounds to letters, naming and sounding the letters of the alphabet. **(CLL)**

> **Cross-curricular links**
> **Stepping Stone**
> ● Choose particular colours to use for a purpose. **(CD)**
> **Early Learning Goal**
> ● Explore colour, texture, shape, form and space in two or three dimensions. **(CD)**

All wrapped up

a	b	c	d	e	f
g	h	i	j	k	l
m	n	o	p	q	r
s	t	u	v	w	x
y	z				

SCHOLASTIC
www.scholastic.co.uk

Invisible words

In this activity the children read a letter that mysteriously arrives through a window. They follow instructions, search for and read, secret messages using magnifying glasses and cover the paper with a paint wash to help them reveal the words.

Early readers enjoy the excitement of the activity and begin to link sounds and letters.
More confident readers read sentences containing some high frequency words and think imaginatively, anticipating what might happen next.

What you need
White paper; gold pen; envelopes; paint washes; paint brushes; white candles; magnifying glasses; a collection of comics containing superheroes appropriate to the children's age.

What to do
● Share the collection of comics, talking about the superhero characters and their exploits.
● Use a candle to write the words *I, will, be, back, on, Friday* on separate pieces of white paper. Place the messages in envelopes labelled, 'SECRET' and hide around the setting. Write a letter to the children, using a gold pen, from a superhero comic character called 'Whizzkid', telling them that he has

left six secret messages around the room, but as the writing is invisible they will have to work out how to read them and then make them into a sentence. Put the letter into an envelope and address it to the children. Ask another member of staff to bring the letter to you with some drama, saying that her window was open and suddenly the letter fluttered in. Build up the children's excitement. Who can it be from? Why wasn't it posted in the usual way? Open and read the letter together.
● Search for the hidden messages around the room. Ask the children to

Learning objectives
Stepping Stones
● Hear and say the initial sound in words and know which letters represent some of the sounds. **(CLL)**
● Begin to recognise some familiar words. **(CLL)**
Early Learning Goals
● Hear and say initial and final sounds in words, and short vowel sounds within words. **(CLL)**
● Read a range of familiar and common words and simple sentences independently. **(CLL)**

try and read the words. But, how can they read them when they are invisible? Ask for their ideas and try out some of them. Suggest that the children become detectives and use the magnifying glasses to help them. Tell them you have an idea that might work and show them how to cover the paper with a paint wash.

● When the words are revealed, ask the children to be detectives trying to work out what each word says by looking at the sounds at the beginning, middle and end of the words, using the magnifying glasses. Read the words together and try and make them into a sentence to see the message that Whizzkid has left them. Eventually make the message, 'I will be back on Friday.'

● Speculate about what will happen on Friday: *Will Whizzkid send another letter? Is he a super hero? Can he fly? What does he look like?*

● When Friday comes you could wrap a packet of biscuits (ensure you check for any food allergies or dietary requirements), or other treat, in gold paper and leave them with a message from Whizzkid for the children to find. Or perhaps, write instructions from Whizzkid for the children to go outside and find a message tied to a balloon, or a message written on the computer or whiteboard. This could complete the activity or you might decide to keep the excitement alive for a few weeks with more messages arriving.

Support and extension
● Write the letters of Whizzkid's name as the hidden messages for younger children.

Help them identify the letter sounds and match the letters to the word Whizzkid in the letter.

● Write sentences as messages for older children, including high frequency words (from the National Literacy Strategy DfES).

Further activities
● Set up one table with white candles and white paper for children to create their own secret messages and another with paint washes and magnifying glasses for other children to reveal and read the messages.

● Encourage the children to look through the collection of comics, talking about the pictures and attempting to read some of the words. Use a highlighter pen to show which words they recognise.

Play link
Fasten a large sheet of paper to a wall and encourage the children to use candles to draw pictures of Whizzkid. Reveal their drawings by painting over the paper with paint washes. **(CD)**

Home link
Suggest that parents or carers let their children choose and buy a comic when out shopping and read this together.

Cross-curricular links
Stepping Stone
● Talk about what is seen and what is happening. **(KUW)**
Early Learning Goal
● Ask questions about why things happen and how things work. **(KUW)**

Take a ticket

**In this activity the children collect, read and make their own tickets
They create choose a form of transport and create a role-play
area for it.**

What you need
Collection of real tickets to
include bus, train, aeroplane,
cinema, theatre and numbered
'queuing' tickets for example
from supermarket delicatessen
counters or a pharmacy; 'Just
the ticket' photocopiable page
25 copied onto card; chairs;
paper; mark-making materials.

What to do
● Show the children the collection of real
tickets and those from the photocopiable
sheet. Ask them when and
why you buy tickets. Read
the words on the tickets
together. What information
does the ticket carry?
● Tell the children that you
want them to choose a
form of transport where
they would need a ticket for
a journey. Arrange chairs to
represent the seats on the
vehicle. Decide on the
destination and make a
sign for the front of the
vehicle and tickets to use.
● Tell the children that they
will need to decide what
information to write on the blank tickets
from the photocopiable sheet. This could
include the form of transport, destination
and price. Depending on the stage of the
children, they can either, write words, make
marks or use a computer. Discuss where
the tickets will be sold, for example, by the
driver on a bus or from a table representing

Early readers read
words on tickets and
signs with adult support
as part of their role play.
More confident readers
make and read their own
bus tickets, routes and
timetables.

Learning objectives
Stepping Stones
● Know information can
be relayed in the form of
print. **(CLL)**
● Begin to recognise
some familiar words.
(CLL)
Early Learning Goals
● Know that print carries
meaning and, in English,
is read from left to right
and top to bottom. **(CLL)**
● Read a range of
familiar and common
words and simple
sentences independently.
(CLL)

a sales desk at an airport. The
children can create their own
props, such as signs, to support
their role play and encourage
reading.

Support and extension
● Support younger children by
participating in the role play
and helping them read the words on the
tickets and signs.
● Older children could link a bus journey to
a favourite story, or the local area, making
their own tickets, bus route and timetable.

Further activity
● Organise and look forward to a special
treat. Set up an area together as a cinema
with a ticket office, torch for the usher, fruit
snacks and drinks for the interval. Make
tickets, choose a favourite film (copyright
permitting) and make posters. Close the
blinds and enjoy the film.

Play link
Set up an area for children to make their
own tickets. Include paper, card, pens,
scissors, stampers, travel
keywords and pictures from
magazines. **(CLL)**

Home link
Ask parents or carers to
save used tickets and bring
them into the setting for the
children to look at. Create a
display incorporating the
tickets and talk about their
different uses.

Cross-curricular links
Stepping Stone
● Engage in imaginative
and role play based on
own first-hand
experience. **(CD)**
Early Learning Goal
● Use their imagination
in art and design, music,
dance, imaginative and
role play and stories. **(CD)**

Just the ticket

Go by bus....

To the shops

Take a plane to

....

BOAT TRIP

See the seals

Party
in the park

Starts at...................

FREE

Our Cinema

Film........
See the film at .
Price: ....
Fruit and drinks on sale

SCHOLASTIC
www.scholastic.co.uk

Mini car sales

In this activity the children share car magazines, information books and websites before making a miniature car showroom. They read and make signs.

What you need

Car magazines; information books about cars; access to the internet if possible; large cardboard boxes; toy cars in various colours; signs from 'Read the signs' photocopiable page 27; paint; brushes; glue stick; polishing cloths.

Learning objectives

Stepping Stones
● Hear and say the initial sound in words and know which letters represent some of the sounds. **(CLL)**
● Know that information can be retrieved from books and computers. **(CLL)**

Early Learning Goals
● Hear and say the initial and final sounds in words, and short vowel sounds within words. **(CLL)**
● Show an understanding of how information can be found in non-fiction texts to answer questions about where, who, why and how. **(CLL)**

Early readers read simple signs with adult support.
More confident readers choose and make their own signs for others to read.

What to do

● As part of a theme about vehicles or moving things share information books, websites and car magazines with the children. Tell the children that you want them to make a car shop or car showroom. Cut the sides of large cardboard boxes to make ramps, wide doors and picture windows. Paint the floor areas with different coloured paints so that the children can match the car to the correct colour bay.
● Read the signs together from photocopiable page 27, encouraging the children to look at the initial sounds as starting points. Discuss why signs are useful and where they should be placed. Let the children decide and glue them in place.
● Allocate a showroom for each child to

manage and ask them to choose cars in the appropriate colour. Give each child a polishing cloth to prepare their cars for the opening of the showroom.

Support and extension

● Limit the number of signs used for younger children, helping them read and understand the signs.
● Older children can choose and make more signs of their own, such as *sales desk, spares* or *workshop*.

Further activity

● Tell the children that you want them to make signs for the room, such as *sand, water* or *books* to make it easier to find things and keep the room tidy. Act as a scribe for younger children and encourage older children to paint or write their own signs.

Play link

Draw a road on the play area and make a *STOP/GO* sign for the children to use to control the ride-on toy traffic. **(CD)**

Home link

Encourage the children to look out for shop or road signs on their way to the setting and tell the group what they have seen.

Cross-curricular links

Stepping Stone
● Display high levels of involvement in activities. **(PSED)**
Early Learning Goal
● Continue to be interested, excited and motivated to learn. **(PSED)**

Read the signs

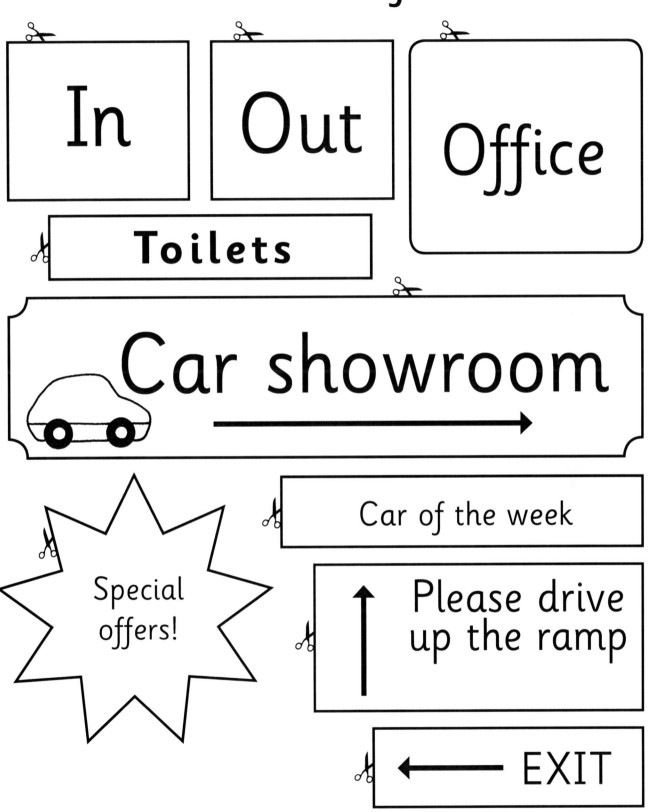

In

Out

Office

Toilets

Car showroom ⟶

Special offers!

Car of the week

↑ Please drive up the ramp

⟵ EXIT

SCHOLASTIC
www.scholastic.co.uk

Game show

The children pretend to be taking part in a television game show as they run around identifying initial sounds.

Early readers learn to recognise the first sound in a word and match the sound to the letter.
More confident readers identify the final sounds in words and recognise *sh*, *ch* and *th* at the beginning of words.

What you need
A bag containing flash cards for six chosen letters and items or pictures with same initial sounds as those used on the letter cards; chalk; a bag of gold coins; a pot of gold (basket of oranges).

What to do
● Ask the children if they have seen game shows on the television. Explain that the contestants play to win prizes. Go outside onto a hard-surfaced play area or into a hall. Tell the children that you are all going to pretend you are taking part in a television game show, trying to win a pot of gold. Divide the children and available adults into four groups and let each group choose a name for itself.
● Draw a circle for each group to stand

inside as their base. Choose six letters as your focus and write these, giant-sized, onto the play area. Explain that the letter shapes make up the 'game board'. Ceremoniously introduce each group in turn. As they are introduced, encourage the children to jump up and down and cheer. Stand on each letter in turn, asking the children to shout the sound of the letter as you do so. Build up the excitement and begin the game.
● As you take a letter card from a bag the children should shout out the sound of the letter and run and stand on the corresponding letter. Remind children of the importance of being

Learning objectives
Stepping Stones
● Distinguish one sound from another. **(CLL)**
● Hear and say the initial sound in words and know which letters represent some of the sounds. **(CLL)**
Early Learning Goals
● Link sounds to letters, naming and sounding the letters of the alphabet. **(CLL)**
● Hear and say initial and final sounds in words, and short vowel sounds within words. **(CLL)**

aware of others when running to the letter shapes, so that everyone remains safe. The first group to stand on the correct letter receives a gold coin and then everyone returns to their bases ready for the next round.

● When the children are confident at recognising the letters, draw an item from the bag, holding it up high. When they see it, the children must run and stand on the letter that corresponds to the initial sound of that object.

● The winners are the group with the most gold coins and they share the pot of gold (a basket of oranges, ensuring to check for any food allergies or dietary requirements).

Support and extension
● Limit the number of letters to two, for younger children.

● Provide more initial letter sounds to choose from for older children or ask them to listen for the final letter sound in words. You could also introduce words beginning with *ch, sh* or *th*.

Further activities
● Provide alphabet cards ('All wrapped up' photocopiable page 21) and a collection of objects and pictures related to a theme

being covered in another area of the curriculum, such as animals. Challenge the children to match the correct letter card to the object with the same initial sound. As children become more confident they can play 'against the clock', setting a timer at the beginning of the activity.

● Set up an 'alphabet table' to help children become familiar with recognising letters and their sounds. Include magnetic letters and boards, alphabet jigsaws, lotto, dice and finger puppets.

Play link
Set up a chalking area outside. Provide coloured chalks, alphabet cards, children's name cards and key words to encourage mark-making and reading. **(CLL)**

Home link
Suggest that parents or carers play a game at home with their children, spotting as many things as possible that begin with the initial sound in the child's name.

Cross-curricular links

Stepping Stones
● Negotiate an appropriate pathway when walking, running or using a wheelchair or other mobility aids, both indoors and outdoors. **(PD)**

● Show respect for other children's personal space when playing among them. **(PD)**

Early Learning Goal
● Show awareness of space, of themselves and of others. **(PD)**

Jelly, Nelly

In this activity children become aware of rhyme. They make up real and imaginary rhyming words, using foods as starting points.

What you need
'Rhyme game' photocopiable page 31 enlarged onto A3 card and copied onto A4 card, and laminated; a copy of *Don't Put Your Finger in the Jelly, Nelly!* by Nick Sharratt (Scholastic Ltd); laminator; paper; whiteboard.

What to do
● Ask the children to think of foods that they particularly like. List these on a large sheet of paper or whiteboard and draw illustrations to provide cues when reading.
● Read aloud the story, *Don't Put Your Finger in the Jelly, Nelly!* by Nick Sharratt. Read it again, this time encouraging the children to contribute the rhyming words. List the words together and ask the children to read them, enjoying the rhymes. Challenge them to think of words that rhyme with the foods on their list. These words can be real or imaginary.
● Read the words on the larger cards together from the photocopiable sheet encouraging the children to use the picture cues to help them. Using the smaller cards, invite the children to play the rhyme game. In this game they turn all the cards faced down. Then one at a time they turn over a card read the word and suggest words that

Early readers begin to hear rhyme and suggest their own rhyming words with support.
More confident readers play with rhyme using more complicated words.

rhyme with it. They can use real or imaginary words but encourage them to notice how the initial sounds change. Add more words as the children become confident with this.

Support and extension
● Help younger children make up rhyming words and repeat the rhyming strings.
● Older children can have fun making up imaginary words to rhyme with more complicated words.

Further activity
● Invite the children to paint pictures of each of the foods named on the cards from photocopiable page 31 and cut a 'finger hole' in each painting. Bind the pictures together to make a book. Encourage the children to make up their own stories as they go through the book, dipping their fingers through the holes into the foods.

Play link
Provide magazines containing pictures of food. Ask the children to choose and cut out the foods that they would like to eat and glue these onto paper plates. Use the plates for a role-play party. **(CD)**

Home link
Suggest that parents or carers include their children in a shopping trip to the supermarket, letting them choose items for a meal.

Learning objectives
Stepping Stones
● Enjoy rhyming and rhythmic activities. **(CLL)**
● Continue a rhyming string. **(CLL)**
● Understand the concept of a word. **(CLL)**
● Begin to recognise some familiar words. **(CLL)**
Early Learning Goals
● Link sounds to letters, naming and sounding the letters of the alphabet. **(CLL)**
● Explore and experiment with sounds, words and texts. **(CLL)**

Cross-curricular links
Stepping Stone
● Display high levels of involvement in activities. **(PSED)**
Early Learning Goal
● Continue to be interested, excited and motivated to learn. **(PSED)**

Discovering reading

Rhyme game

cake	jelly	pear
jam	bun	bread
egg	cheese	milk

Reading without realising

Reading environment

Jungle cafe

Creating a busy jungle cafe designed for animals will provide an exciting role-play area with lots of reading opportunities in the form of signs, badges, menus, lists and posters. Encourage the children to help you make the cafe and keep the area as a focus for several weeks.

Early readers begin to take an interest in print and realise that it carries meaning.
More confident readers have many opportunities to read independently for information in a lively role-play setting.

What you need
An area large enough to set up a role-play cafe; collection of animal stories, animal pictures and information books about jungle animals; animal masks; empty buckets, newspaper and plaster bandage (to make rocks); 'At the Jungle Cafe' photocopiable page 35 enlarged to A3 with cards laminated; tables; cash register; money; telephone; pen; cooker or cardboard box; kitchen utensils; ice-cream tubs; salt dough; plain fabric (for table cloths); paint; large sheets of paper; green paper; crepe paper; animal shaped sponges; badges for the characters; cookery books; laminator.

What to do
These activities are designed to be taught over several sessions.

Introducing the idea
Ask the children what they would expect to find in a cafe and list their ideas on a large sheet of paper.

Learning objectives
Stepping Stones
● Show interest in illustrations and print in books and print in the environment. **(CLL)**
● Know information can be relayed in the form of print. **(CLL)**
Early Learning Goals
● Know that print carries meaning and, in English, is read from left to right and top to bottom. **(CLL)**
● Read a range of familiar and common words and simple sentences independently. **(CLL)**

Read the list together. Explain that you want them to make a cafe to play in, but it will be a cafe for jungle animals, not for people. Share the collection of animal books and pictures with the children and ask them to name some jungle animals. Make a list of their suggestions. *Rumble in the Jungle* by Giles Andreae (Orchard Books) has lively rhymes and excellent illustrations to use as starting points. Tell the children that you know four animals who are regular visitors to the cafe, they are snake, tiger, chimpanzee and crocodile. Either underline these if they are on the list, or add them to it. Ask the children to put circles around the names of four more animals they would like to include in the role-play cafe.

Setting the scene
Include the children in the planning and creating of the jungle cafe, using their ideas wherever possible. The following suggestions can be used or adapted:
● Paint a *Jungle cafe* sign to hang at the entrance to the role-play cafe area.
● Set up tables for the customers or eating areas on the floor. Make rocks by covering buckets with newspaper and wet plaster bandage. When dry, paint grey.
● Use one table as the cash desk with cash register and money. Provide a telephone, pen and message pad (see next point and photocopiable sheet).
● Use the photocopiable sheet to make the

Menus, Customer's order form, Clean up checklist, Telephone message pad and Business cards. Read the menus with the children and invite them to make the appropriate food from salt dough. Bake the dough at a low temperature. When cold, paint and varnish the food and store in labelled ice-cream tubs.
● Set up the kitchen area with cooker (this could be a cardboard box), pans, plates, cutlery and cookery books. Make signs such as: *Please wash your hands, Hot!* or *Wet floor.* Add the salt dough food.
● Invite the children to paint and cut out very large, colourful pictures of animals to decorate the cafe walls. Add tall trees, brightly-coloured flowers, birds and insects. Help the children to make labels for the animals and plants. Make vines by plaiting lengths of green crepe paper and draping them from the ceiling to the walls.
● Make plates in the shapes of giant leaves cut from green paper and laminated.
● Print lengths of plain fabric using animal-shaped sponges, to make tablecloths.
● Provide animal masks for the customers
● Make *Open* and *Closed* signs, price lists and a *Specials* board.

Role play and reading
● Allocate roles when children are playing in the jungle cafe. Make badges for the children, to include the animal names, cook, waiter or waitress, cashier and cleaner.

33

Model the roles of each character and include an adult in the role-play area whenever possible, to maintain the role play and to support and encourage reading.

● Each role has different reading requirements:

● *Animal customers* read the signs, Business cards (on the tables), Menu and Specials board before ordering.

● *The waiter or waitress* reads the Specials board and Customer's order notepad, when taking the customer's order.

● *The cook* reads the orders, cookery books and signs.

● *The cleaner* reads the Clean up checklist, recording whether or not tasks are completed.

● *The cashier* reads the bill, writes and reads messages.

Support and extension

● Play alongside younger children, encouraging and supporting them with the role play and reading.

● Invite older children to make their own menus, lists and posters and be more independent during the role play.

Further activities

● To maintain children's interest in the role-play area, arrange particular events, such as an unexpected visitor, a photographer's visit or a birthday party for one of the animals. Introduce different animals such as insects or birds. Make new name badges and revise the menu to cater for the tastes of the new clientele and create new reading opportunities.

● Encourage the children to use non-fiction books and CD-ROMs to find out more information about jungle animals and help them make an information book of their own. They can display it in the Jungle Cafe.

Play link

Cover a basket with fake fur fabric, adding soft toys and animal story books such as *Handa's Surprise* by Eileen Browne (Walker Books). Put it in the reading corner and encourage the children to read the stories to the animals. **(CLL)**

Home link

Involve parents or carers in the children's activities by inviting them to visit the cafe at the beginning or end of a session.

Cross-curricular links

Stepping Stones
● Display high levels of involvement in activities. **(PSED)**
● Notice what adults do, imitating what is observed and then doing it spontaneously when the adult is not there. **(CD)**
● Introduce a story line or narrative into their play. **(CD)**

Early Learning Goals
● Continue to be interested, excited and motivated to learn. **(PSED)**
● Use their imagination in art and design, imaginative and role play and stories. **(CD)**

At the Jungle Cafe

Jungle cafe

Telephone messages

Jungle cafe

Clean up checklist

1. Clear the tables   YES/NO
2. Wash the pots   YES/NO
3. Wipe the tables   YES/NO

Jungle cafe

Customer's order

- ☐ Froggy burgers
- ☐ Lizard stew
- ☐ Wiggly worms
- ☐ Ants on toast
- ☐ Wild pig pie
- ☐ Jungle curry
- ☐ Juicy leaves
- ☐ Honey seed tart
- ☐ Banana mountain
- ☐ Red flower cake
- ☐ Coconut milk
- ☐ Green berry pop

Jungle cafe

MENU

Froggy burgers

Lizard stew

Wiggly worms

Ants on toast

Wild pig pie

Jungle curry

Juicy leaves

Honey seed tart

Banana mountain

Red flower cake

Coconut milk

Green berry pop

Jungle cafe

**The food is yummy –
Come and fill your tummy**

Toy workshop

A lively workshop area where children repair large and small toys provides a stimulating environment in which the children will want to read a range of words and begin to use writing to record information and communicate. While they play they will be reading labels, signs, order forms, names and telephone numbers.

Early readers begin to realise that print carries meaning and have opportunities to read as an integral part of role play.
More confident readers read and write for a real purpose and make their own resources providing further reading opportunities.

What you need
Notepads made using 'Fix it' photocopiable page 39; large outdoor toys; small toys; tables; play tools, toolboxes and tool belts; overalls; plastic bottles, jugs and containers; shoe boxes; labels; sticky tape; string; telephone; telephone directory; till; money; diary, notepad and pen; chipboard; clips; toy catalogues; paint; paper; sponges and cloths; boxes; badges; magnifying glasses; card; scissors; glue; dustpan and brush; computer (optional).

What to do
These activities are designed to be taught over several sessions.

Introducing the idea
Tell the children that you want them to help make a workshop where they can pretend to fix things that are broken. These could be large outdoor ride-on toys or small toys. Examine some toys that need repairing and talk about what is wrong with them. If possible arrange a visit

Learning objectives
Stepping Stones
● Show interest in illustrations and print in books and print in the environment. **(CLL)**
● Know information can be relayed in the form of print. **(CLL)**
Early Learning Goals
● Know that print carries meaning and, in English, is read from left to right and top to bottom. **(CLL)**
● Read a range of familiar and common words and simple sentences independently. **(CLL)**

to a local shop that repairs bicycles or household appliances. List together things that will be needed in the workshop. These could include a workbench, tools, spare parts, oil and a telephone. Read the list together.

Setting the scene

● Plan the area you will use and incorporate the children's ideas as you go along. Involve the children in making the resources so that they feel the area is really their own.

● Allow space for a large area for the ride-on toys, a table as a workbench for the small toys and another table for the office.

● Paint a shop sign and paint or use a computer to make labels for the different areas such as, *Big Toys*, *Small Toys*, and *Office*.

● For the big toys area, provide overalls, toolboxes, tool belts, play tools, a dustpan and brush.

● Stick labels onto small plastic bottles or jugs, saying oil, water, and cleaner. Make a storage unit for these by removing the flaps from cardboard boxes, gluing and taping them together. Paint the unit, add sponges and cloths, label the shelves and add a sign saying *Please keep tidy*.

● Make a 'shadow board' for tools. Attach clips to a piece of chipboard and attach the play tools to the board using the clips. Draw around their outlines with a pen. Label each tool. Secure the board to a wall at child height. When the tools are removed the children can see where to replace them.

● Make a checklist notepad for the mechanics repairing the large toys and a customer order form using the photocopiable sheet.

● For the small toys area provide a box containing small play tools, magnifying glasses, card, scissors, sticky tape and string. Make a check list of these items to keep in the box.

● Label a box *Toys to mend* and another *Mended toys*.

● Include a box of toy catalogues and pictures of toys, for reference.

● In the office area, put a telephone, notepad and pen, till with pretend money, diary, telephone directory, a list of names and telephone numbers, Customer order form (see photocopiable sheet) and an Open/Closed sign.

Role play and reading

● Remind the children that it is safe to play with these tools and bottles, but they should never play with tools or bottles they find anywhere else.

● Talk to the children about the different areas in the workshop and what they can do in each one. Explain that when they play in an area they will have a particular role.

Make badges showing the different roles, such as Big toys mechanic, Small toys mechanic, Office worker and Customer.

● Customers will bring toys that need mending, fill in the Customer order form and take the toy to the correct area for repair. When the toy is repaired, the customer takes the order form to the office and pays the bill.

● Read signs, labels and photocopied resources together. Explain to the children how to complete the Big toys checklist and Spare parts orders. Play alongside the children, modelling the different roles, supporting the play, looking at how things work and encouraging reading.

● The different areas will have different reading opportunities:

● *In the big toys area*, the mechanics read labels, the Big toys checklist, and read and write on the Customer order forms.

● *In the small toys area*, the assistants read labels, the Spare parts order forms and refer to toy catalogues.

● *In the office* the staff read the Customer orders, Spare parts order, names and telephone numbers.

Support and extension

● Simplify the role-play to just the big toys area and office for younger children. Participate in the role play, encouraging the children to read using the picture cues.

● Older children can make more resources themselves such as toy and tool catalogues, simple time sheets and rotas.

Further activities

● Make one A4-sized book, with the title *Small Toys* and one A3-sized book with the title *Big Toys*. Ask the children to make a collection of favourite toys in different sizes and sort them into two sets, large and small. Invite the children to choose a toy from one of the sets and make a labelled drawing to add to the appropriate book.

● Make a story basket of picture books about toys that the children can read independently.

Play link

Set up a toymaker's studio. Provide assorted art materials suitable for creating models of toys. Encourage the children to make their own models and display these in the workshop. **(KUW)**

Home link

Plan a special story time for parents and carers to share the books with their children when they come to collect them.

Cross-curricular links
Stepping Stone
● Show an interest in why things happen and how things work. **(KUW)**
Early Learning Goal
● Ask questions about why things happen and how things work. **(KUW)**

Fix it

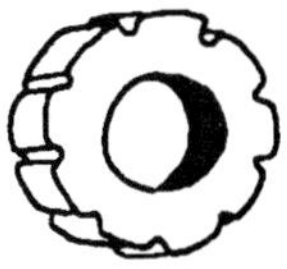

Big toys
Checklist

1. Wheels ☐
2. Seat ☐
3. Pedals ☐
4. Handlebars ☐
5. Steering wheel ☐

All mended ☐

Not mended ☐

Customer order

Please mend my

_____

Name:

_____

Please pay

£ _____

Spare Parts Order

Parts	How many?
nuts	
bolts	
nails	
screws	

Please send quickly!

SCHOLASTIC
www.scholastic.co.uk

Let's find out

Immerse the children in the excitement of a television channel by setting up this vibrant learning environment in which they can select a 'zone', find things out and read non-fiction materials.

Early readers enjoy the excitement of the new area and begin to understand that they can use books and digital resources to help them find information.
More confident readers read signs, labels and questions. They find information from a wide variety of sources and design and make their own resources for others to read and share.

What you need
Very large cardboard box; small cardboard boxes; tables; remote control from 'Which zone?' photocopiable page 43; thick card; painting materials; polystyrene ball; dowelling; collection of natural objects; magnifying glasses; books and pictures appropriate to each zone; construction kits; squared paper; coloured pencils; coloured Cellophane; colour paddles; programmable toys; computer; scissors; chairs; pencils; paper; coloured card; photographs of buildings; remote control toys.

What to do
This activity is designed to be taught over several sessions.

Introducing the idea
This reading environment is ideal to prepare and set up as an exciting surprise for children. It involves the children in finding out things for themselves and using non-fiction resources. They can be involved in adding to the area, adapting and making their own activities once it is in use. Build up the suspense before you create the area, by telling the children that when they come into the setting the next day, there will be a big surprise for them with lots of exciting things to do. When the day arrives, tell the children that they are going to step inside a television that is tuned to the 'Find out

Learning objectives
Stepping Stones
● Show interest in illustrations and print in books and print in the environment. **(CLL)**
● Know information can be relayed in the form of print. **(CLL)**
● Know that information can be retrieved from books and computers. **(CLL)**
Early Learning Goal
● Show an understanding of how information can be found in non-fiction texts to answer questions about where, who, why and how. **(CLL)**

channel'. When they are inside there are lots of interesting things to do and find out.

Setting the scene

● The area you use can be as large or small as the space available. Ideally you should be able to create four or five zones within the 'Find out channel' area.

● Partition an area for the 'Find out channel' and make an entrance, using if possible, a giant cardboard box (used for large electrical appliances) to represent a television. Cut out a wide 'screen' large enough for the children to step through and paint the box to look like a television. Use photocopiable page 43 to make the television remote control and glue to a piece of thick card. Make signs saying, *News zone, Nature zone, Building zone, Colour zone* and *Toy zone*.

● News zone: create a news desk by setting up a table with a microphone made from a polystyrene ball pushed onto a piece of dowelling, pens and paper. Put out two chairs for the news readers and make stand-up labels for the children to write their names – real or imaginary – for their role as news reader. Make a desk sign saying *ON AIR*.

● Nature zone: collect natural objects that are of interest because of their texture or pattern, such as a pineapple, fir cone, seed

heads, bark, pebbles or shells. Make labels for each item and display on a table labelled *Nature zone*. Include relevant non-fiction books and pictures, magnifying glasses, paper and pencils.

● Building zone: set up a table with construction kits, photographs and books showing different types of buildings in different parts of the world. Make cards with the pictures and names of different buildings on them for the children to read. Include squared paper and coloured pencils, to encourage drawing and labelling.

● Colour zone: provide sheets of coloured Cellophane and colour paddles, so that the children can see how new colours can be created. Write the colour words on pieces of coloured card. On a separate table nearby, set up a painting area for the children to experiment in mixing their own colours. Write questions on card cut into the shape of paint pots or brushes such as: *Can you make purple? Can you make orange? Can you make green?*

● Toy zone: section off an area of floor where the children can use programmable and remote control toys. Provide labelled boxes for storing the toys. Provide cards with directional words: *forwards, backwards, left, right* and see if the children can move the toys in these ways. There could also be

obstacles to negotiate such as under the chair, behind the cushion and so on.

Role play and reading

● Explain to the children that before they enter the 'Find out channel' they must decide which zone they want to visit and press the appropriate button on the remote control. Introduce the children to the zones by showing them how to use each area, reading the signs, labels and information together. Include an adult working in the area to support investigation and reading.
● The leaning opportunities in the zones are:

● *In the News zone* the children read the signs and depending on the stage they are at, either make marks or write their own news and read 'on air' as newsreaders.

● *In the Nature zone* the children use their senses as they examine natural objects, make drawings, read labels and find information in non-fiction books.

● *In the Building zone* children use construction kits, find information from books about different types of building. They read the names of buildings and make their own drawings and label them.

● *In the Colour zone* the children experiment in making colours, read

questions and the colour names.
● *In the Toy zone* children use ICT as they learn to control toys. They read labels, returning the toys to the correct boxes.

Support and extension

● Support younger children with their reading and ask questions to encourage them to find things out.
● Challenge older children to set up a new zone of their own, collecting resources, making signs, labels and posing questions.

Further activities

● Take the Nature zone outside. Provide a backpack containing magnifying glasses, a digital camera, notebooks and pencils to encourage children to explore their environment and record their findings.
● Make a Time zone, by collecting replicas of toys from the past (possibly obtained from a local museum service) or by asking parents to loan their childhood toys (make sure they are labelled), photographs and books of old vehicles, clothes children wore, toys and seaside holidays.

Play link

Make a Wet zone outside, using the water tray, water pumps, water mills, plastic jugs and watering cans to enable the children to find out about water for themselves. **(KUW)**

Home link

Encourage the children to invite their parents to visit the 'Find out channel' with them at the end of the session.

Cross-curricular links

Stepping Stones
● Complete a simple program on the computer and/or perform simple functions on ICT apparatus. **(KUW)**
● Show curiosity, observe and manipulate objects. **(KUW)**
● Examine objects and living things to find out more about them. **(KUW)**

Early Learning Goals
● Find out about and identify the uses of everyday technology and use information and communication technology and programmable toys to support their learning. **(KUW)**
● Find out about and identify, some features of living things, objects and events they observe. **(KUW)**

Which zone?

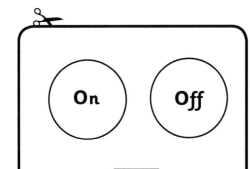

On   Off

1

News zone

2

Nature zone

3

Building zone

4

Colour zone

5

Toy zone

■SCHOLASTIC
www.scholastic.co.uk

Bears in the forest

Together you create an exciting reading environment with a teddy bear theme. The children create and enter a forest and share the great variety of teddy bear stories by favourite authors.

Early readers are introduced to books, the joys of stories and rhyming language.
More confident readers begin to recognise rhyme, read common words and become aware of story structure.

What you need

Three books by Jez Alborough: *Where's My Teddy?*, *My Friend Bear* and *It's the Bear!* (all Walker Books); bear stories; bear poems; non-fiction books about bears; pictures of bears; a selection of teddy bears; cardboard box; basket; picnic basket; paper; paints; collage materials; beanbags or floor cushions; fabric in 'forest colours'; picnic rugs; display grass or green fabric; fir cones; twigs; crayons; bear-coloured paper; card; dowelling; red ribbon; 'Teddy bears' photocopiable page 47 enlarged to A3 and laminated; small-world boy; scissors; pencils.

What to do

These activities are designed to be taught over several sessions.

Introducing the idea

Show the children the three books by Jez Alborough and read *Where's My Teddy?* (This is also available as a Big Book that is great for sharing with a group.) Talk about the characters and the events in the story. Enjoy the rhythm of the words with the children, inviting them to say the rhyming names of the characters: *Eddy, Freddy* and *Teddy*. Explain that you want them to help set up an area like the forest in the story, where they will be able to pretend that they are the characters in the book. Look at the illustrations together and discuss how they can create the forest.

Learning objectives
Stepping Stones
● Show awareness of rhyme and alliteration. **(CLL)**
● Begin to recognise some familiar words. **(CLL)**
Early Learning Goals
● Hear and say initial and final sounds in words, and short vowel sounds within words. **(CLL)**
● Read a range of familiar and common words and simple sentences independently. **(CLL)**

Setting the scene

● Paint tall thin trees, mixing shades of brown for the trunks. Cut these out and use them to cover the walls of the reading area to create a forest. Add branches that stretch up to and along the ceiling. Make leaves using collage materials and hang them from the branches, to create an enclosed woodland effect.

● Cover part of the floor with display grass (obtainable from greengrocers or supermarkets) or a green rug and add fir cones and twigs.

● Create an inviting reading area by providing seating using beanbags or floor cushions draped with fabric in 'forest colours'. Place the basket of books about bears near the seating and arrange a selection of teddy bears on a picnic rug.

● Invite the children to make up a 'Eddy, Freddy and Teddy' box containing the three books by Jez Alborough, a large teddy bear with a smaller bear, a small-world boy to represent Eddy and a very small teddy bear as Freddy. Make name tags using card labels to hang around the toys' necks. Paint the names on the side of the box.

● Ask the children to paint each character in the story. Cut out and mount their paintings onto card and attach these to pieces of dowelling to make puppets. Cover a table with green fabric or display grass for

the children to use when producing a puppet show.

● Create an area to encourage mark-making and early writing. Provide pieces of bear-coloured paper, scissors, pencils and coloured crayons. Include labels and red ribbon for the children to make name labels for their own bears. Write rhyming words from the story and rhyming CVC words on cards for the children to read and copy.

● Make a 'Sizes' table. Use the bears from the photocopiable sheet for the children to order and match to the labels. Add a variety of teddy bears for the children to order by size.

Role play and reading

● Work with the children in each area, modelling the way to use the materials and enjoy the activities. Limit the number of children in the area at any one time to ensure that they have time and space to read and explore the activities. Include an adult working in the area, whenever possible, to maintain the quality of play.

● The different areas provide different learning opportunities:

  ● *In the reading area* children learn how to handle books, choose favourite stories and begin to understand about characters and the elements of stories.

  ● *The Eddy, Freddy and Teddy box,*

Reading without realising

provides an opportunity for the children to read the books and retell the stories using some of the rhyming language. They read the names on the box and make and read name tags for the characters.

● *The puppets* provide opportunities for children to get into character and try out the language they have heard in the stories and to sequence events.

● *The mark-making area* gives children the chance to record their ideas and thoughts on paper and to read and write labels and rhyming words.

● *The sizes area* provides opportunities for discussions about the size of the bears, ordering the bears by size and reading labels.

Support and extension

● Spend time sharing the books with younger children, giving them the chance to talk about the stories, characters, rhyming words and illustrations.

● Encourage older children to read with you, pointing to the words and identifying and enjoying the sounds of the rhyming words.

Further activities

● Read *It's the Bear!* by Jez Alborough, to the children. Prepare a picnic similar to the one in the story. Take rugs to sit on and set off on a walk, going outside and ending in the 'forest'. Read the story again with the children enacting the story. Enjoy the picnic together.

● Read *My Friend Bear* by Jez Alborough, to the children. Ask them to pick out the rhyming words and enjoy their sounds. Talk about times when the children may have felt lonely and how our friends are important to us.

Play link

Tell the children that it is 'snuggle up' time. They need to find a teddy bear to cuddle, a story book and somewhere comfortable to sit in the forest where they can snuggle up and read their story to the bear. **(CLL)**

Home link

Ask the children to bring a teddy bear into the setting, to talk about and take into the forest at 'snuggle up' time.

Cross-curricular links

Stepping Stones
● Order two or three items by length. **(MD)**
● Play alongside other children who are engaged in the same theme. **(CD)**

Early Learning Goals
● Use developing mathematical ideas and methods to solve practical problems. **(MD)**
● Use their imagination in art and design, imaginative and role play and stories. **(CD)**

Teddy bears

	Tiddly teddy
	Small teddy
	Big teddy
	Gigantic teddy

SCHOLASTIC

www.scholastic.co.uk

Giant's world

Children will enjoy creating an exciting giant's room after listening to the story of *Jack and the Beanstalk*. They discover words and pictures hidden behind leaves, read giant words and write on giant notepads. They live the story as they participate in role play.

Early readers are introduced to an environment full of print in unexpected places. **More confident readers** sequence a story and enjoy reading for different purposes.

What you need

An area for the giant's room; a copy of *Jack and the Beanstalk* by Nick Sharratt and Stephen Tucker (Macmillan Children's Books) or other version of the story; collection of different versions of the story; Big Books of traditional stories; paints; card; paper; green crepe paper; large felt-tipped pens; large rubber; long ruler; large desk; wooden chair; key; mug; basket; tin; flipchart; easel; cereal boxes; giant flashcards showing keywords from the story; story sequence cards (see *Setting the scene*); 'A giant book' photocopiable page 51; clothes for role play; badges showing characters' names; props for storytelling.

What to do

These activities are designed to be taught over several sessions.

Introducing the idea

Share the *Jack and the Beanstalk* story with the children. Talk about the characters and sequence the events in the story. Ask the children to describe the giant's room and the size of the objects found there. Use the flashcards naming the objects in the room and read together. Tell the children that they are going to make a room for the giant together.

Learning objectives

Stepping Stones
● Begin to recognise some familiar words. **(CLL)**
● Begin to be aware of the ways stories are structured. **(CLL)**
Early Learning Goals
● Read a range of familiar and common words and simple sentences independently. **(CLL)**
● Show an understanding of the elements of stories, such as main character, sequence of events and openings. **(CLL)**

Setting the scene

● Make the giant's room with the children. Encourage them to be active in suggesting ideas and talking about the way they want the room to look. Incorporate their ideas into the design as much as possible.

● Section off an area with furniture or display boards. Paint *Fee, Fi, Fo, Fum!* in large letters and hang at the entrance to the room. Add big furniture and items such as a wooden chair, table, key, plate and mug.

● Make a giant's bookshelf and add 'books' made by covering cereal boxes and writing the titles of traditional stories on the 'spines'.

● Display the giant flashcards in the boxes plus other books or CD-ROM versions of *Jack and the Beanstalk.*

● Make a beanstalk stretching from floor to ceiling, by twisting green crepe paper or using rope. Make enormous leaves and paint in shades of green using rollers or sponges. Laminate some of the lower leaves and attach them to the wall so that the children can 'lift the flap' to find labelled pictures of items from the story underneath.

● Invite the children to draw the characters from the story, ensuring that the giant is very tall and Jack is very small. Paint and cut out the figures and attach to the walls of the giant's room.

● Decorate a large cardboard box that is big enough to hold the fairy tales in Big Book format. Add the title *Giant's books – Have a Look!*

● Create a giant desk area to include notepads made from A3 paper labelled *Giant's lists, Giant's phone book* and *Giant's diary.* Add large felt-tipped pens stored in a tin labelled *Giant's pens,* a long ruler and large rubber. Include a flipchart and easel, if available and label as *Giant's notes.*

● Make numbered cards, telling the story. Fix these around the room, in sequence:

   ● *Jack sold the cow for magic beans.*
   ● *A bean grew into a very tall beanstalk.*
   ● *Jack climbed the beanstalk.*
   ● *Jack went into the giant's house.*
   ● *Jack took the giant's gold coins.*
   ● *The giant said, 'Fee, Fi, Fo, Fum!'*
   ● *Jack ran home to his mum.*

● Provide a box of role-play clothes and badges for each of the characters.

● Fill a basket with props that the children have made or drawn, such as golden eggs, gold coins, harp, hen and a bag of beans plus the corresponding words for the children to match. (Take extra care when using small parts with young children.)

● Use the photocopiable sheet to make booklets for the children to complete.

Role play and reading

● Sit in the giant's room with the children

and explain how to use the area. Model the roles of each character as the children are playing and read the flashcards, labels and numbered story cards together. Include an adult in the role-play area whenever possible to support the role play and encourage reading.

● *The flashcards, labels and badges* provide opportunities for reading familiar words and those linked to the story.

● *The 'lift the flap' leaves* encourage reading, using picture cues.

● *The numbered cards* help children to sequence the story and read common and related words.

● *The giant's desk area* provides opportunities for reading and writing on a large scale.

● *The basket of props and corresponding words* encourages imaginative play and reading, as children match the cards to the objects.

● *The boxes of books and CD-ROMs* enable the children to share different versions of the story and read other traditional stories in book form or on screen.

● *The booklets* provide the opportunity for the children to make and read their own simple books. Fold the books and draw a picture of Jack on the front cover, the giant in the centre of the book and themselves on the back cover.

Cross-curricular links

Stepping Stone
● Introduce a storyline or narrative into their play. **(CD)**
● Play alongside other children who are engaged in the same theme. **(CD)**

Early Learning Goal
● Use their imagination in art and design, imaginative and role play and stories. **(CD)**

Support and extension

● Help bring stories alive for younger children by participating in the role play and encouraging them to read simple words.

● Older children can use the flash cards and story sequence cards to help them make up their own stories.

Further activities

● Organise a Beanstalk growing competition. Invite each child to plant a runner bean in the garden or in a large pot. The children should label the pots with their names and care for the plants.

● Make a collection of potted plants and tell the children that you want them to order the plants by height. Encourage use of the appropriate language such as taller, tallest, shorter, shortest, the same as.

Play link

Provide a 'beanstalk kit', consisting of green bricks, green paper, scissors and sticky tape. Challenge the children to make the tallest beanstalk they can, cutting out and attaching leaves to the 'stalk'. **(CD)**

Home link

Send home a story book for each child to share with their parent or carer.

A giant book

...I am just right!

Jack is small...

Jack and the beanstalk

by ....

The Giant is

BIG

↓

(look inside)

SCHOLASTIC

www.scholastic.co.uk

Reading around

Reading faces

Children learn to 'read' the emotions shown in facial expressions and the words associated with them.

What you need
'Making faces' photocopiable page 53 enlarged to A3 with cards laminated.

What to do
● Tell the children to look around the setting for something to read and bring it to share in a circle. Remark that everything they have brought contains letters and words, which is what we usually need when we want to read. But can we read anything without using words? Listen to their ideas and then ask if they can 'read' your face and tell how you are feeling. Make sad, happy, cross or surprised facial expressions for them to read. Talk about times when they have felt these and other emotions.
● Encourage the children to take turns in making faces for the rest of the group to read. Introduce the laminated, 'Making faces' cards (from the photocopiable sheet). Ask the children to look at the cards and say what the face tells them about how each child is feeling. Point out the words under the pictures and read these together. Tell the children that when you hold up a card you want them to read the words, using the picture cues, and then make the appropriate face.

Early readers begin to understand that print carries meaning and use picture cues to help them read words.
More confident readers use picture cues initially and then begin to read words independently.

Support and extension
● Limit the number of faces that younger children read to happy, sad and cross.
● As older children gain confidence in recognising the words, ask them to read the cards without illustrations and make the appropriate faces.

Further activity
● Make two sets of the 'Making faces' cards. Shuffle and place the cards face down on the table. The children take it in turns to turn over two cards, trying to find a matching pair.

Play link
Provide play dough or clay, paints and paper and a set of the 'Making faces' cards. Encourage the children to make faces from these materials showing different emotions. **(CD)**

Home link
Suggest that parents or carers play a 'How am I feeling?' game with their children. By 'reading' each others faces.

Learning objectives
Stepping Stones
● Know information can be relayed in the form of print. **(CLL)**
● Begin to recognise some familiar words. **(CLL)**
Early Learning Goals
● Know that print carries meaning and, in English, is read from left to right and from top to bottom. **(CLL)**
● Read a range of familiar and common words and simple sentences independently. **(CLL)**

Cross-curricular links
Stepping Stones
● Express needs and feelings in appropriate ways. **(PSED)**
● Use body language, gestures, facial expression or words to indicate personal satisfaction or frustration. **(CD)**
Early Learning Goals
● Have a developing awareness of their own needs, views and feelings. **(PSED)**
● Express and communicate their ideas, thoughts and feelings. **(CD)**

Making faces

happy	sad	cross
scared	surprised	excited
happy	sad	cross
scared	surprised	excited

Read your body

In this activity the children 'read' the messages their bodies are sending them, becoming aware of their own needs in regard to keeping healthy. They read and match parts of a sentence.

What you need
Laminated cards from 'My body says' photocopiable page 55 enlarged to A3; white tack; board.

What to do
● Go outside with the children and tell them to run around the field or play area and stop when they feel tired. When the children stop and rest, ask them how they knew it was time to stop. Talk to the children about the fact that they 'read' the message that their body was giving them, which was, 'I am tired – stop and rest'.
● Ask the children to think of other times when they have read messages from their bodies. For example: 'I am hungry – time to eat' or 'I am thirsty – time to drink'. Explain that acting on these messages helps to keep us healthy.
● Read the 'My body says' cards with the children, helping them to find the correct pairs. Use white tack to stick the *When I say…* and *My body says…* headings next to each other on a board. Challenge the children to stick the cards under the appropriate headings.

Early readers read words with support, using picture cues to help them.
More confident readers play a matching game with a partner, reading words and sentences independently.

Learning objectives
Stepping Stones
● Know information can be relayed in the form of print. **(CLL)**
● Begin to recognise some familiar words. **(CLL)**
Early Learning Goals
● Know that print carries meaning and, in English, is read from left to right and top to bottom. **(CLL)**
● Read a range of familiar and common words and simple sentences independently. **(CLL)**

Support and extension
● With younger children, read and sort the cards together, encouraging them to use the picture cues when reading.
● Older children can use the A4 set of cards, and play the matching game at a table with a partner.

Further activity
● Stop the children at key times during the day, such as before lunch or after exercise and ask them if they can read any messages that their bodies are sending them and what they need to do in order to keep healthy.

Play link
Encourage role play by providing a collection of soft toy animals for the children to look after, checking for example if they are hungry, thirsty or tired and using available props to support their play. **(CD)**

Home link
Keep parents and carers informed about health initiatives in the setting, such as the healthy snacks you provide or the free availability of water to drink.

Cross-curricular links
Stepping Stone
● Show some understanding that good practices with regard to exercise, eating, sleeping and hygiene can contribute to good health. **(PD)**
Early Learning Goal
● Recognise the importance of keeping healthy and those things which contribute to this. **(PD)**

My body says

When I say...	My body says...
I am hot –	cool me down.
I am cold –	warm me up.
I am tired –	stop and rest.
I am hungry –	time to eat.
I am thirsty –	time to drink.
I am sleepy –	time for bed.
I have a pain –	tell a grown up.

Reading without realising

SCHOLASTIC
www.scholastic.co.uk

Read the rhythm

In this lively, musical activity the children learn to 'read the rhythm' as they become aware of the rhythm in music and words. They march, dance, play instruments and join in with action songs.

What you need

A wide variety of dance music such as jive, rock 'n' roll, waltz, rap, big band, marching band, ballet; music player; laminated cards from 'In the groove' photocopiable page 57.

What to do

● Tell the children that as soon as they hear music playing you want them to listen to the beat and move in time to the music. Start by playing a piece of music with a strong marching beat and join in with the children as they march around.

● Tell the children to make a circle and copy your actions as the music is playing. March on the spot, turn, clap, tap your shoulders or pat your knees in time to the music.

● Make up simple jingles together that emphasise the rhythm, such as:

March, march, march, march.

Do not stop!

March, march, march, march.

To the shop!

● Talk about the actions they have performed. Read and match the sentence cards and illustrations from photocopiable page 57.

Learning objectives

Stepping Stones
● Enjoy rhyming and rhythmic activities. **(CLL)**
● Show awareness of rhyme and alliteration. **(CLL)**
● Begin to recognise some familiar words. **(CLL)**

Early Learning Goals
● Hear and say initial and final sounds in words, and short vowel sounds within words. **(CLL)**
● Read a range of familiar and common words and simple sentences independently. **(CLL)**

Early readers begin to respond to and become aware of rhythm and read some words using picture cues.
More confident readers enjoy the rhythm of music, songs and words. They read simple sentences and make up their own sequences of actions.

● Repeat the activity with different types of music.

Support and extension

● Join in with the dancing to support and encourage younger children to be aware of rhythm. Help them to read the action cards by looking at the pictures for clues.

● Older children can clap the rhythm as they say the syllables in their names or other words.

Further activity

● Give each child an instrument they can strike to make a sound. Encourage them to 'read the rhythm' and join in by playing the instruments in time to the music as they sing *The Grand Old Duke of York*.

Play link

Encourage children to respond to rhythm by providing an open space, music player, musical instruments and a collection of varied music for them to select. **(CD)**

Home link

Encourage parents to sing and say rhymes with their children as part of their everyday activities. You could send home a sheet of songs and rhymes that the children enjoy.

Cross-curricular links

Stepping Stones
● Respond to sound with body movement. **(CD)**
● Begin to move rhythmically. **(CD)**
● Tap out simple repeated rhythms and make some up. **(CD)**
Early Learning Goal
● Match movements to music. **(CD)**

In the groove

I can march.	
I can skip.	
I can turn.	
I can clap.	
I can tap.	

SCHOLASTIC
www.scholastic.co.uk

Read the picture

Use the fun picture of a busy street scene to encourage children to 'read' information from a picture, noticing and talking about people at work and recognising humorous situations.

What you need
'In the picture' photocopiable page 59 enlarged to A3; whiteboard or paper.

What to do
● Show the children the enlarged copy of the photocopiable sheet. Comment that although there are some words on the signs in the picture, there is no story or written information to explain what the picture is about or what is happening. Can they 'read' the picture without any words?
● Challenge the children to describe the environment and work out what is happening in the picture. Make a list of the jobs they see people doing and include simple drawings next to the words to act as picture cues. Read the words together.
● Have the children noticed the dogs in the picture? Ask them to tell you what the dogs are doing and count how many there are altogether. Read and talk about the signs in the picture.

Support and extension
● Work with a very small group of younger children, encouraging and supporting them as they talk about the things they notice.
● Challenge older children to speculate

Early readers learn to look carefully at pictures and find information.
More confident readers find and interpret information from a picture, speculating about what may be happening.

why things are happening and what will happen next.

Further activity
● Make a large picture of a busy street scene, with each child contributing a drawing of a person engaged in an activity, to add to the picture. 'Read' the finished picture together.

Play link
Provide a selection of information books about people at work and some items to encourage role play such as a bucket and cloth, play gardening tools or a postman's bag and letters. **(CD)**

Home link
Suggest that parents or carers encourage their children to notice at least three things that are happening as they travel to the setting each day.

Learning objectives
Stepping Stones
● Show interest in illustrations and print in books and print in the environment. **(CLL)**
● Know information can be relayed in the form of print. **(CLL)**
● Use talk to connect ideas, explain what is happening and anticipate what might happen next. **(CLL)**
Early Learning Goals
● Know that print carries meaning and, in English, is read from left to right and top to bottom. **(CLL)**
● Use talk to organise, sequence and clarify thinking, ideas, feelings and events. **(CLL)**

Cross-curricular links
Stepping Stone
● Show an interest in the world in which they live. **(KUW)**
Early Learning Goal
● Observe, find out about and identify features in the place they live and the natural world. **(KUW)**

In the picture

Reading symbols

Thinking about celebrations is the focus of this activity as children 'read' symbols they associate with particular celebrations or religious festivals.

What you need
An attractive box tied with a ribbon, containing laminated symbol cards (from 'Time to celebrate' photocopiable page 61, enlarged to A3); a collection of birthday cards designed for different members of a family; card; coloured pencils or pens.

> **Early readers** begin to link a symbol with a particular object or event. **More confident readers** draw and 'read' their own symbols.

Learning objectives
Stepping Stone
● Begin to recognise some familiar words. **(CLL)**
Early Learning Goal
● Read a range of familiar and common words and simple sentences independently. **(CLL)**

What to do
● Challenge the children to think of occasions when they celebrate family events. Make a list of occasions such as engagement, wedding, birth, birthday, passing tests and anniversaries and read this together. Also talk about celebrating religious festivals relevant to the children and time of year, such as Christmas, Hanukkah and Divali.
● Show the children the special celebrations box with the symbol cards inside it. Ask them to 'read' the symbols and tell you what each one means to them. The symbols may mean different things to different children and form the basis of a discussion. For example, the candle could represent Hanukkah to one child and Christmas or a birthday to others.
● Talk about the fact that we send cards on special occasions and to mark religious festivals. Show the children the collection of birthday cards and read the messages together. Tell the children that you want them to make a birthday card for someone

special and keep it in the celebrations box. They can choose the greeting and write 'Love from…' inside the card.

Support and extension
● Focus on one celebration with younger children, making for example, a birthday box.
● Older children can draw their own symbols to represent aspects of celebrations and add these to the celebrations box.

Further activity
● Ask the children to tell you about special foods they have when celebrating their birthdays. Make a model birthday cake by covering a tin with paper, painting it and adding candles. Keep the cake in the celebrations box. When a child has a birthday take out the cake and all sing 'Happy Birthday'.

Play link
Make a role-play box to include dressing up items for a wedding and pictures or books about weddings. Include items representing more than one religion. **(CD)**

Home link
Share the celebrations box with parents and carers and invite them to add appropriate photographs or artefacts to the box.

Cross-curricular links
Stepping Stones
● Describe significant events for family or friends. **(KUW)**
● Gain an awareness of the cultures and beliefs of others. **(KUW)**
Early Learning Goal
● Begin to know about their own cultures and beliefs and those of other people. **(KUW)**

Time to celebrate

Read the time

Children learn that they can read the time from a clock face. They sequence special times in their day, reading the corresponding words.

What you need
'What's the time?' photocopiable page 63 enlarged to A3 and laminated; a teaching clock; a collection of assorted clocks; cards.

What to do
● Go outside with the children and play 'What's the time, Mr Wolf?' Ask the children to think of particular times that are important to them each day. List these on cards and read them together. Narrow the list down to breakfast time, lunchtime, teatime and bedtime. Tell the children that everyone has different times for getting up and having their meals, but you have a list of Mr Wolf's times.

● Show them the enlarged clocks (from the photocopiable sheet). Read the times on the clocks and the words below, using the picture cues on the clock faces.

● Ask four children to hold the clocks and stand in the correct sequence. Read the words together. Take the opportunity to develop use of the language of time, such as: after, before, next, later.

● Show the children the collection of clocks and encourage them to read the numerals. Using the teaching clock, make the 'o'clock' times together, linking the times to the children's day.

Learning objectives
Stepping Stones
● Know information can be relayed in the form of print. **(CLL)**
● Begin to make patterns in their experience through linking cause and effect, sequencing, ordering and grouping. **(CLL)**
Early Learning Goals
● Know that print carries meaning and, in English, is read from left to right and top to bottom. **(CLL)**
● Use talk to organise, sequence and clarify thinking, ideas, feelings and events. **(CLL)**

Early readers become aware that they do things at a particular time each day and that time can be read from a clock face as well as in words.
More confident readers learn to read the 'o'clock' times and words associated with time.

Support and extension
● Talk to younger children about specific times in the day and let them enjoy playing with the clocks.
● Older children can learn to make and read the 'o'clock' times on the teaching clock.

Further activity
● Glue large copies of the three clocks showing meal times onto sheets of A3 paper. Discuss foods eaten at breakfast, lunch and teatime and invite the children to draw these, sticking their pictures onto the appropriate sheets.

Play link
Provide a simple 'home corner' (including clocks) for children to role play their day from getting up to going to bed. **(CD)**

Home link
Suggest that parents or carers talk to their children about the order of events in their family's day.

Cross-curricular links
Stepping Stone
● Display high levels of involvement in activities. **(PSED)**
Early Learning Goal
● Be confident to try new activities, initiate ideas and speak in a familiar group. **(PSED)**

What's the time?

SCHOLASTIC

In this series:

ISBN 978-0439-94499-1

ISBN 978-0439-94515-8

ISBN 978-0439-94556-1

ISBN 978-0439-94555-4

To find out more, call: 0845 603 9091
or visit our website www.scholastic.co.uk